THE LITTLE BOOK OF

SILLY

WHAT DO YOU CALL JOKES

ROBERT MYERS

OTHER BOOKS BY ROBERT MYERS

365 Knock-Knock Jokes

www.amazon.com/author/rmyers

To Ellen

thank you

CONTENTS

SAY WHAT?

What do you call something that stays
on the ground but never gets dirty?
A shadow.

What do you call having your
grandma on speed dial?
Instagram.

What do you call a woman on the arm
of a banjo player?
A tattoo.

What do you call two monkeys that
share an Amazon account?
Primemates.

What do you call it when your parachute doesn't open?
Jumping to a conclusion.

What do you call Kris Kringle when he goes on his wife's health insurance?
A dependent Claus.

What do you call an apology written in dots and dashes?
Remorse code.

What do you call an American drawing?
A Yankee Doodle.

What do you call a grocery clerk in Peking?
A Chinese checker.

What do you call a blonde who dyes
her hair brown?
Artificial intelligence.

What do you call a skeleton that went
out in freezing temperatures?
A numb skull.

What do you call a pessimistic
Mexican?
A Mexicant.

What do you call a cow jumping over
barbed wire?
Utter destruction.

What do you call a group of 5
chickens and 10 crows?
A murder most fowl.

What do you call a snobby criminal walking down the steps?
A condescending con descending.

What do you call the lights on Noah's ark?
Flood lights.

What do you call a lady insect that sucks blood?
A Ms. Quito.

What do you call a cow that doesn't give milk?
A milk dud.

What do you call a snake with a great personality?
A snake charmer.

What do you call a car that never stops running?
Cargo

What do you call dangerous precipitation?
A rain of terror.

What do you call someone who says they know all the words to AULD LANG SYNE?
A liar.

What do you call a vampire who lives in a kitchen?
Count Spatula.

What do you call a music teacher with problems?
A trebled man.

What do you call a crying camel?
A humpback wail.

What do you call an unpredictable,
out of control photographer?
A loose Canon.

What do you call an argument
between two electric companies?
A power struggle.

What do you call a person who plays
basketball in a suit and tie?
A gym dandy.

What do you call a pounding
headache?
A temple tantrum.

What do you call a witch on the beach?
A sandwich.

What do you call a pig that likes to take off her clothes?
Bacon Strips.

What do you call a trendy pig?
Calvin Swine.

What do you call a snake that's employed by the government?
A civil serpent.

What do you call a fat psychic?
A four-chin teller.

What do you call a basement full of liberals?
A whine cellar.

IT'S RAINING CATS AND DOGS

What do you call a dog that licks an electrical socket?
Sparky.

What do you call a painting of a cat?
A pawtrait.

What do you call the cat that was caught by the police?
The purrpatrator.

What do you call a frozen dog?
A pupsicle.

What do you call a cat crossed with a fish?
A catfish.

What do you call a large dog that meditates?
Aware wolf.

What do you call it when a cat wins in a dog show?
A CAT-HAS-TROPHY!

What do you call a cat that wears make up?
A glamourpuss.

What do you call a cross between a matador and a cute little puppy dog?
A cocker Spaniard.

What do you call young dogs playing
in the snow?
Slush puppies.

What do you call an extremely large
cat?
A MEOW-SIVE-CAT.

What do you call a sleeping
Rottweiler?
Anything you like, just very quietly!

What do you call a cat that can rough
the great outdoors?
A survival kit.

What do you call a blind dog?
A dog that usually barks up the wrong
tree.

What do you call a cat with eight legs
that likes to swim?
An octopussy.

What do you call a great dog
detective?
Sherlock Bones.

What do you call a cat that eats
lemons?
A sourpuss.

What do you call a dog that wins a
race?
A weiner.

What do you call Lassie with a rose in
her mouth?
A cauliflower.

What do you call a cat on ice?
One cool cat.

What do you call a cat that gets
anything it wants?
Purr-suasive.

What do you call a dog with a Rolex?
A watch dog.

What do you call a dog owned by
Dracula?
A blood hound.

What do you call a cross between a
dog and a
frog?
A croaker Spaniel.

What do you call a cat that likes to tell jokes?
A witty kitty.

What do you call a meeting with numerous dogs present?
A bow-wow pow-wow.

What do you call a cat that can put together furniture from Ikea?
An assembly kit.

What do you call a loving cat bite?
A cat nip.

What do you call a dog in the middle of a muddy road?
A mutt in a rut.

What do you call a cross between a
pit bull and a computer?
A lot of bites.

What do you call a boring dog?
A dull-mation.

What do you call an old Tom cat?
Grand-Paw.

What do you call a dog wearing jeans
and a T-shirt?
A plain clothes police dog.

What do you call a cat that ate a
duck?
A duck-filled-fatty-puss.

What do you call a dog's kiss?
A pooch smooch.

What do you call a black Alaskan dog?
A dusky husky.

What do you call a dog's spaghetti?
Poodle's noodles.

What do you call cats that live in igloos?
Eskimeows.

What do you call a cross between a cat and a ghost?
A scaredy cat.

What do you call it when a dog is choking on a piece of jewelry?
A diamond in the ruff.

What do you call a dog with a fever?
A hot dog.

What do you call a cat police force?
Claw enforcement.

What do you call a cross between a
cat and a parrot?
A carrot.

What do you call a dog with a
surround system?
A sub-woofer.

What do you call a nutty dog in
Australia?
A dingo-ling.

What do you call a dog that designs
buildings?
A bark-itect.

What do you call a dog magician?
A labracadabrador.

What do you call a dog with royal
blood?
A regal Beagle.

What do you call it when one cat sues
another cat in court?
A clawsuit.

What do you call a cross between a
bird, a car, and a dog?
A flying carpet.

What do you call a nine day old dog
in Russia?
A puppy.

What do you call a cat race?
A meow-athon.

What do you call a cross between a
Doberman and a hyena?
No idea, but if it laughs, I join in!

What do you call a dog that is left-
handed?
A south paw.

What do you call a dog with no legs?
It doesn't matter what you call him, he
still won't come!

What do you call a cold dog sitting on
a bunny?
A chili dog on a bun.

What do you call a cross between a
ball and a
cat?
A fur ball.

What do you call a cat that loves to
bowl?
An alley cat.

What do you call a cat that can
address the media?
A press kit.

What do you call a cat that gives up?
A quitty.

What do you call a cat with no
money?
A paw-purr.

What do you call a dog that enjoys
taking bubble
baths?
A shampoodle.

What do you call a sheep dog's tail
that can tell tall stories?
A shaggy dog tale.

What do you call a happy Lassie?
A jolly collie.

What do you call dogs that dig up
ancient artefacts?
Barkaeologists.

What do you call a dog that can use
the toilet?
A poo-dle.

What do you call a fluffy male cat
asleep on a
bed?
A Himalayan.

What do you call a cat that smells good?
A Purr-fumed feline.

What do you call it when a cat is super-stylish?
Haute-cat-ture.

WHAT'S IN A NAME?

What do you call two men standing in
a window?
Kurt and Rod.

What do you call a girl with a
sunlamp on her
head?
Tanya.

What do you call a guy with no arms
or legs who lies on the floor?
Matt.

What do you call a computer that sings?
Adelle.

What do you call a man who likes gardening?
Herb.

What do you call a camel with no humps?
Humphrey.

What do you call a girl who is leisurely and
aimless?
Wanda.

What do you call a Scottish thief?
Rob.

What do you call a man with no arms
or legs hanging on a wall?
Art.

What do you call a woman with a
tortoise on her
head?
Shelley.

What do you call a lady magician?
Trixie.

What do you call a boy who sticks his
right arm down a lion's throat?
Lefty.

What do you call a guy with a rubber
toe?
Roberto.

What do you call a Spaniard who
can't find his
car?
Carlos.

What do you call a man with a crane
on his head?
Derek.

What do you call a science fiction
hero who happens to be a water fowl?
Duck Rogers.

What do you call a woman who
throws her bills
on the fire?
Bernadette.

What do you call a Chinese woman
with a food mixer on her head?
Brenda.

What do you call a man with a toilet
on his head?
John.

What do you call a woman with a cat
on her head?
Kitty.

What do you call a girl with a big
head?
Heddy.

What do you call a woman sitting in a
bath of martinis?
Olive.

What do you call a man with a map
on his head?
Miles.

What do you call a man with a
wooden head?
Edward.

What do you call a man with three
wooden heads?
Edward Woodward.

What do you call a man with four
wooden heads?
I don't know but Edward Woodward
would!

What do you call a girl who has a lot
of spare change?
Penny.

What do you call a guy who was out
all night on the grass?
Dewey.

What do you call a guy who is not
crazy?
Norm.

What do you call a girl who is very
conceited?
Mimi.

What do you call a girl who is an
astronomer?
Stella.

What do you call a man who likes to
hike a great deal?
Walker.

What do you call a woman who likes
to push around a little cart?
Dolly.

What do you call a guy who is all
feet?
Archie.

What do you call a woman with a
breeze on her head?
Gail.

What do you call a man who lives on
a back
street?
Ali.

What do you call a man who breaks
dishes?
Chip.

What do you call a boy with mucus in
his nose and throat?
Fleming.

What do you call a man in denial?
Very wet.

What do you call a man who's been
mauled by a tiger?
Gord.

What do you call a man who's been
struck by lightning?
Rod.

What do you call a man who's always
there when you need him?
Andy.

What do you call a boy who likes to
read?
Red.

What do you call a man who votes
things down all the time?
Vito

What do you call a man in debt?
Owen.

What do you call a man who ties
ribbons for a living?
Beau.

What do you call a man who hits a
baseball over the fence?
Homer.

What do you call a man who always
wins?
Victor.

What do you call a girl who likes sweets?
Candy.

What do you call a man who likes to ring doorbells?
Buzz.

What do you call a girl who likes to play hide-and-go-seek?
Heidi.

What do you call a man who likes to wear all types of hats?
Cap.

What do you call a girl who has to be helped around a lot?
Carrie.

What do you call a man who breaks
into
houses?
Jimmy.

What do you call a man with a car
number plate on his head?
Reg.

What do you call a guy who makes
loudspeakers?
Mike.

What do you call a man with a spade
on his head?
Doug.

What do you call a man without a
spade on his
head?
Douglas.

What do you call a girl who likes to
work in a garden?
Fern.

What do you call a man who likes all
kinds of
cars?
Otto.

What do you call a woman who is
always taking people to court?
Sue.

What do you call a man who loves
cats?
Bartholo-meow.

What do you call a man with a toilet
on his head?
Lou.

What do you call a woman with two
toilets on her head?
Lulu.

What do you call a man who is very
adventurous?
Darin.

What do you call an Indian who
doesn't laugh
very much?
Minnehaha.

What do you call a woman who is in
charge of the water faucet?
Flo.

What do you call a girl who makes
hamburgers?
Patti.

What do you call a man who jokes all the time?
Josh.

What do you call a man who is a lookout for the Coast Guard?
Seymour.

What do you call a man who grows things in the garden?
Bud.

What do you call a man with legal documents on his head?
Will.

What do you call a man who drives a truck?
Laurie.

What do you call a man with a kilt on his head?
Scott.

What do you call a man in a pothole?
Phil.

What do you call a girl with a tennis racket on her head?
Annette.

What do you call a man who comes through the letterbox?
Bill.

What do you call a man in a pile of leaves?
Russell.

What do you call a man in a pot?
Stu.

What do you call a woman with one
leg longer than the other?
Eileen.

HAPPY HOLIDAYS

What do you call a bankrupt Santa?
Saint-nickel-less.

What do you call someone who
doesn't believe
in Father Christmas?
A rebel without a Claus.

What do you call sweet potatoes that
are very
outspoken?
Candid yams.

What do you call a nervous witch?
A twitch.

What do you call a cross between a
monster and
a pig?
Frankenswine.

What do you call a forgetful rabbit?
A hare-brain.

What do you call the bells on Santa's
sleigh?
Kringle bells.

What do you call a ghost with a
broken leg?
A hobblin' goblin.

What do you call a cross between a
rabbit's foot
and poison ivy?
A rash of good luck.

What do you call a cross between a
snowman and
a vampire?
Frostbite.

What do you call people who are
afraid of Santa
Claus?
Claustrophobic.

What do you call a witch's garage?
A broom closet.

What do you call the song sung at a
snowman's
birthday party?
Freeze a jolly good fellow!

What do you call a cross between an
apple and a
Christmas tree?
A pine-apple.

What do you call a bunny with a large
brain?
An egghead.

What do you call a cross between a
witch and a
snowman?
A cold spell.

What do you call a mischievous egg?
A practical yolker.

What do you call a running turkey?
Fast food.

What do you call a cross between a
Yule log and a
duck?
A fire quacker.

What do you call a bunny with
money?
A millionhare.

What do you call a shark that delivers
toys at Christmas?
Santa Jaws.

What do you call an egg from outer
space?
An Egg-stra-terrestial.

What do you call a cross between a
turkey and an octopus?
Enough drumsticks for everybody!

What do you call a bunny with fleas?
Bugs Bunny.

What do you call a cross between a
turkey and a banjo?
A turkey that plucks itself.

What do you call a bull that gets
castrated on December 31?
An un-happy new steer.

What do you call an obnoxious
reindeer?
Rude-olph.

What do you call a cross between a
ghost and a torn sheet?
A holy terror.

What do you call a letter sent up the chimney on Christmas Eve?
Blackmail.

What do you call a door to door ghost salesman?
A dead ringer.

What do you call Santa Claus with unfolded clothes?
Kris Wrinkle.

What do you call a cross between a ghost, a dog and a rooster?
A cockatoo.

What do you call a scary looking reindeer?
A cariboo.

What do you call a dancing ghost?
Polka-haunt-us.

What do you call an over-caffeinated turkey?
A per-key.

What do you call a cross between a sheep and a cicada?
Baa Humbug!

What do you call a rabbit with the sniffles?
A runny bunny.

What do you call a fat bearded man who slides down your chimney in December?
A thief who is out of shape.

What do you call a cross between a turkey and a bell?
A bird that has to wring its own neck.

What do you call a turkey on the day after?
Lucky.

What do you call the age of a Pilgrim?
Pilgrimage.

What do you call an Easter Bunny that gets kicked out of school?
Egg-spelled.

What do you call a cross between a bunny and
a bee?
A honey bunny.

What do you call Santa when he takes a break?
Santa Pause.

What do you call a rude turkey?
A jerk-key.

What do you call a frog hanging from the ceiling?
Mistletoad.

What do you call a kind and considerate monster?
A complete failure.

What do you call a very tired Easter egg?
Eggs-austed.

What do you call a stuffed animal?
You, after Thansgiving!

What do you call a skeleton that cleans?
The grim sweeper.

What do you a turkey that has no feathers?
Thanksgiving dinner.

What do you call a snowman with a six-pack?
An abdominal snowman.

ZOO PARADE

What do you call an elephant that
doesn't matter?
An irrelephant.

What do you call a monkey that loves
to eat potato chips?
A chipmonk.

What do you call a group of killer
whales playing musical instruments?
An orca-stra.

What do you call an alligator that
makes others fight?
An instigator.

What do you call a solitary shark?
A lone shark.

What do you call a cross between an
elephant and a rhino?
An elephino.

What do you call a zebra with no
stripes?
A horse.

What do you call a rooster that wakes
you up at the same time every
morning?
An alarm cluck.

What do you call six green apes?
A bunch of gr-apes!

What do you call an elephant in a phone booth?
Stuck.

What do you call a bear with no socks on?
Bare-foot.

What do you call an alligator that sneaks up and bites you from behind?
A tailgator.

What do you call a three-footed aardvark?
A yardvark.

What do you call a snake that becomes a Canadian law officer?
A Mountie Python.

What do you call a turtle that flies?
A shellicopter.

What do you call an exploding ape?
A baboom.

What do you call a rabbit that works
in a bakery?
A yeaster bunny.

What do you call a bear with no
money?
Bear-oke.

What do you call a well balanced
horse?
Stable.

What do you call a cow that overacts?
A ham ham.

What do you call an ant that likes to
be alone?
An independ-ant.

What do you call a whale that talks
too much?
A blubber mouth.

What do you call a cow on the
barnyard floor?
Ground beef.

What do you call a bee that is having
a really bad hair day?
A Frisbee.

What do you call an elephant that
flies?
A jumbo jet.

What do you call a cow that eats your grass?
A lawn moo-er.

What do you call a sleeping werewolf?
An unaware wolf.

What do you call a pig that is wrong.
Mistaken bacon.

What do you call a pony with a cough?
A little hoarse.

What do you call a feminine cow?
A dairy queen.

What do you call a rabbit that is really cool?
A hip hopper.

What do you call an ant that skips school?
A truant.

What do you call someone who is always stealing birds?
A birdler.

What do you call a crafy pig?
CunningHam

What do you call 99 rabbits stepping backwards?
A receding hair line.

What do you call two young married spiders?
Newly webs.

What do you call a deer with no eyes?
No idea.

What do you call a deer with no eyes and no
legs?
Still no idea.

What do you call a very rude bird?
A mockingbird.

What do you call an operation on a
rabbit?
A hare cut.

What do you call an ant with frog's
legs?
An antphibian.

What do you call a bear with no
teeth?
A gummy bear.

What do you call a sick eagle?
Illegal.

What do you call a pig that's not fun
to be around?
A boar.

What do you call a horse that enjoys
arts and
crafts?
A hobby horse.

What do you call a 100-year-old ant?
An antigue.

What do you call a seagull that flies
over the
bay?
A bagel.

What do you call a monkey that wins the World
Series?
A chimpion.

What do you call a person who kills leopards?
A spot remover.

What do you call a pig that drives recklessly?
A road hog.

What do you call a hen that's staring at a lettuce?
Chicken sees a salad.

What do you call a sleeping bull?
A bulldozer.

What do you call a duck with fangs?
Quakula.

What do you call a short sunburned
outlaw riding
a horse?
Little Red Riding Hood.

What do you call an ant that lives
with your great
uncle?
Your great ant.

What do you call a pig with 3 eyes?
Piiig.

What do you call a chicken at the
North Pole?
Lost!

What do you call a sad bird?
A bluebird.

What do you call a bee born in May?
A Maybe.

What do you call a pig with skin problems?
A wart-hog.

What do you call two elephants on a bicycle?
Optimistic.

What do you call an owl with a deep voice?
A growl.

What do you call a really strong cow?
Beefy.

What do you call a medicine that you give to pigs?
Oinkment.

GRAB BAG

What do you call a sleepwalking nun?
A roamin' Catholic.

What do you call the little rivers that
flow into
the Nile?
Juve-Niles.

What do you call a dentist who's good
at adding
or taking away teeth?
A mouthematician.

What do you call a thieving alligator?
A crookodile.

What do you call a cow in an earthquake?
A milkshake.

What do you call a dentist in the army?
A drill sergeant.

What do you call a person who draws amusing pictures of motor vehicles?
A car-toonist.

What do you call a pan spinning through space?
An unidentified frying object.

What do you call a man who spent all summer at the beach?
A tangent.

What do you call two birds in love?
Tweet hearts.

What do you call two witches who
share a broom?
Broom mates.

What do you call a cross between an
apple and a shellfish?
A crab apple.

What do you call a nosy pepper?
Jalapeno business.

What do you call a fly without wings?
A walk!

What do you call people who only
pretend to be composers?
Sym-phonies.

What do you call a can opener that
doesn't work?
A can't opener.

What do you call a cross between a
sorceress and a millionaire?
A very witch person.

What do you call it when it rains
chickens and ducks?
Fowl weather.

What do you call a missing parrot?
A polygon.

What do you call a priest who
becomes a lawyer?
Father-in-law.

What do you call a test tube that graduates from high school?
A graduated cylinder.

What do you call cheese that isn't yours?
Nacho cheese.

What do you call a fake noodle?
An Impasta.

What do you call a girl who has three boyfriends named William?
A bill collector.

What do you call a stupid mummy?
A dummy mummy.

What do you call an ice cream truck operator?
A sundae driver.

What do you call an IT teacher who touches up his students?
A PDF file.

What do you call someone doing 2000 pounds of laundry?
Washing-ton.

What do you call a wheel made of iron?
A ferrous wheel.

What do you call a cross between a city bird and
a frog?
We're not sure – but it will probably be pigeon-toad.

What do you call a stolen yam?
A hot potato.

What do you call a really quiet armed crusader?
A silent knight.

What do you call a computer hero?
A screen saver.

What do you call the most important tennis match on Mars?
The UFOpen.

What do you call a dream in which polar bears are attacking you?
A bitemare.

What do you call a pirate who skips class?
Captain Hooky.

What do you call a funny mountain?
Hill-arious.

What do you call a diseased criminal?
A leper-con.

What do you call a sad tree?
A weeping willow.

What do you call a person who doesn't have all his fingers on one hand?
Normal. Fingers are supposed to be on two hands.

What do you call a vampire's favorite fruit?
A neck-tarine!

What do you call a cross between a telephone and a pair of pants?
Bell-bottoms.

What do you call a pastor in Germany?
A German Shepherd.

What do you call people who are in favor of tractors?
Protractors.

What do you call CHILDREN OF THE CORN'S father?
Pop corn.

What do you call someone who puts poison in a person's corn flakes?
A cereal killer.

DINOSAURS

What do you call a dinosaur that is
elected to
Congress?
Rep. Tile.

What do you call a dinosaur with an
extensive vocabulary?
A thesaurus.

What do you call a dinosaur as tall as
a house, with long sharp teeth, and 12
claws on each foot?
Sir!

What do you call a dinosaur that's a noisy sleeper?
A Bronto-snorus.

What do you call a dinosaur at the rodeo?
A Bronco-saurus.

What do you call Tyrannosaurus rex when it wears a cowboy hat and boots?
Tyrannosaurus tex.

What do you call it when a dinosaur gets into a car accident?
A Tyrannosaurus wreck!

What do you call Harry Potter's dinosaur?
The dinosorcerer.

What do you call a dinosaur that is
always on time?
A Pronto-saurus.

What do you call a Stegosaurus with
carrots in its ears?
Anything you want, it can't hear you!

What do you call a dinosaur with one
eye?
Eye-saur.

What do you call a Tyrannosaurus
that talks and talks and talks?
A Dinobore!

What do you call a dinosaur that
never gives up?
Try and try and try and Try-ceratops.

What do you call a dinosaur fossil
that doesn't want to work?
Lazy bones.

What do you call a dinosaur that eats
its vegetables?
A Brocileasparus.

What do you call a Triceratops that
scores its first goal?
A Dino-score!

What do you call a dinosaur with a
foul mouth?
A Bronto-swore-us.

What do you call a dinosaur that eats
fireworks?
A Dino-mite.

What do you call a cross between a pig and a dinosaur?
Jurassic Pork.

What do you call a dinosaur with stripes?
A Zebra-saurus.

What do you call a dinosaur that does yoga?
Tyrannosaurus Flex.

What do you call a cross between a dog and a dinosaur?
A mutta-saurus.

What do you call a dinosaur that left its armor out in the rain?
A Stegosau-rust.

What do you call a Japanese dinosaur?
Godzilla. Geez, where have you been?

What do you call a scared dinosaur?
A nervous rex.

What do you call the dinosaur that fought Santa Anna with Daniel Boone?
Alamo-saurus.

What do you call a a dinosaur's puppy?
Rex!

What do you call a cross between a T-rex and a sombrero?
A Tyrannosaurus Mex.

What do you call a T-rex that waits tables?
A Dinersaur.

What do you call a polite dinosaur?
A Pleaseyosaur.

What do you call a dinosaur with bad eyesight?
Do-you-think-he-saurus.

What do you call a T-rex that hates losing?
A saur loser.

What do you call a baby dinosaur?
A Wee-rex.

What do you call a thin T-rex?
Ano-rex.

What do you call a dinosaur after a breakup?
breakup?
A Tyrannosaurus-ex.

BONANZA!

What do you call two guys from
Mexico playing basketball?
Juan on Juan.

What do you call one cow spying on
another?
A steak out.

What do you call a South American
girl who is always in a hurry?
Urgent Tina.

What do you call a big pile of kittens?
A meowntain.

What do you call the ghost of a chicken?
A poultry-geist.

What do you call a ten foot high stack of frogs?
A toad-em pole.

What do you call a dirty chicken that crosses the road and crosses back?
A dirty double crosser!

What do you call a king who is only twelve inches tall?
A ruler.

What do you call an illegally parked frog?
Toad.

What do you call an Arabian dairy farmer?
A milk sheik.

What do you call a sad coffee?
Despresso.

What do you call a man who is always wiring for money?
An electrician.

What do you call two cat burglars?
A pair of knickers.

What do you call a big fish that makes you an offer you can't refuse?
The Codfather.

What do you call an overweight pumpkin?
A plumpkin.

What do you call a cow with a twitch?
Beef Jerky.

What do you call a policeman in bed?
An undercover detective.

What do you call a man with no body
and just a nose?
Nobody nose.

What do you call a cross between a
vegetable and our first president?
George Squashington.

What do you call a belt with a watch
on it?
A waist of time.

What do you call a boy with a
dictionary in his pants?
Smartie Pants.

What do you call it when Batman skips church?
Christian Bale.

What do you call a Vicar on a moped?
Rev.

What do you call a story about a broken pencil?
Pointless.

What do you call a robot that always takes the longest route?
R2 Detour.

What do you call a cross between a robot and a tractor?
A trans-farmer.

What do you call a cross between one principal and another principal?
I wouldn't do it – principals don't like to be crossed!

What do you call a police strike?
A cop-out.

What do you call a girl guide in Belgium?
A Brussels scout.

What do you call a fantasy show about basketball?
Hooper-natural.

What do you call a small wound?
A short cut.

What do you call a gentleman who
shaves 20 times a day?
A barber.

What do you call a cow that has just
given birth to a baby?
Decalfinated.

What do you call a snail on a ship?
A snailor.

What do you call a parade of German
mercenaries?
A Hessian procession.

What do you call a pretty girl using a
broom?
Sweeping Beauty.

What do you call a bicycle built by a chemist?
Bike-carbonate of soda.

What do you call a herd of cattle with a sense of
humor?
Laughing stock.

What do you call a crazy spaceman?
An astronut.

What do you call the fruits of anger?
Bad apples.

What do you call a little boy's messy room?
A toynado.

What do you call a fake stone in Ireland?
A sham-rock.

What do you call a humorous knee?
Fun-ny!

What do you call a fashion conscious crab?
A snappy dresser.

What do you call a lineman's kid?
A chip off the old blocker.

What do you call a song sung in a car?
A car-tune.

What do you call an Italian referee?
A Roman umpire.

What do you call a test given to a criminal?
A con-test.

What do you call Jesse James when he has the flu?
A sick shooter.

ANIMAL FARM

What do you call a group of racist
white chickens?
Coo Clucks Clan.

What do you call a laundromat for
pigs?
Hogwash.

What do you call a cow that's failed at
everything its ever tried?
A mooser.

What do you call a funny cow?
A cowmedian.

What do you call a horse that likes to stay up
late?
A night mare.

What do you call an elephant that can fly?
A propellephant.

What do you call a bear anarchy?
A panda-monium.

What do you call a duck that gets straight A's
in school?
A wise quacker.

What do you call a cranky cow?
Mooooooooody.

What do you call a horse wearing
venetian
blinds?
A zebra.

What do you call elephants that
swim?
Swimming trunks.

What do you call a bear with no arms
and no
legs?
An ambulance! This is no time for
jokes.

What do you call a pig thief?
A hamburglar.

What do you call a monkey with a
wand and a broomstick?
Hairy Potter.

What do you call a duck that steals?
A robber duck.

What do you call a Spanish pig?
Porque.

What do you call a monkey that's in
charge of its tree?
A branch manager.

What do you call two ducks and a
cow?
Quackers and milk.

What do you call an evil baby cow?
A veal-lin.

What do you call a boy named Ryder
who likes to ride a horse's back?
HORSE BACK RYDER.

What do you call a elephant that's pleasingly graceful and stylish in appearance?
An elegant.

What do you call a caretaker of chickens?
A chicken tender.

What do you call a bear that never wants to grow
up?
Peter Panda.

What do you call a cow with no toes?
Lac-toes intolerant.

What do you call a noisy horse?
A herd animal.

What do you call five-hundred
elephants at a
concert?
The audience.

What do you call a chicken that
crossed the road?
Suicidal.

What do you call a wet bear?
A drizzly bear.

What do you call a pig that does a
great deal of charity work?
A philanthropig.

What do you call a baby monkey that
takes after its mother?
A chimp off the old block.

What do you call a duck on drugs?
A quackhead.

What do you call a pig that plays
baseball?
A ball hog.

What do you call a monkey that can't
keep a
secret?
A blab-boon.

What do you call a duck that loves
fireworks?
A firequacker.

What do you call a horse that's been
around the world?
A globe-trotter.

What do you call a baby elephant in water?
A little squirt.

What do you call a bear with extreme mood swings?
A bi-polar bear.

What do you call a horse with two legs?
A horse without two legs.

What do you call elephants that ride on trains?
Passengers.

What do you call a group of chickens clucking in unison?
A hensemble.

What do you call a bear that pushes all the other bears into the pool?
The dry bear.

What do you call a pig with no legs?
A groundhog.

What do you call a monkey that works in a call center?
A who-rang-utang.

What do you call a rude duck?
A duck with a quackitude.

What do you call a pig that can't mind its own business?
A nosey porker.

What do you call a monkey with eight legs?
A spider monkey.

What do you call a duck's rear end?
Buttquack.

What do you call a half-horse, half-politician creature?
A Senataur.

What do you call an elephant covered in mud?
DIRTY!

What do you call someone who is caught stealing a chicken?
A chicken pot pirate.

What do you call a bear that practices dentistry?
A molar bear.

What do you call a cow's facial hair?
A moostache.

What do you call a highly critical horse?
A nay-sayer.

What do you call a bear that always brings up unpleasant things?
A bearer of bad news.

What do you call a very intelligent pig?
A Swinestein.

What do you call chopped up monkey pieces?
Rhesus pieces.

What do you call a bloody pig?
HAMorrhage.

What do you call a duck with a Ph.D?
Ductor.

What do you call a dictatorial cow?
Moosilini.

What do you call an explosive horse?
Neigh-palm.

What do you call a naked bear?
A bare.

What do you call a gay cow?
A gay cow.

What do you call a big mean polar
bear?
Don't call it anything – just RUN!

What do you call a bunch of chickens
in a two-door car trying to overthrow
the government?
A coop coupe coup.

THIS AND THAT

What do you call a bagel that can fly?
A plain bagel.

What do you call a fruit playing the guitar?
A jam session.

What do you call a math rock band fronted by Al Gore?
Algorithm.

What do you call the pants of a five-legged monster?
A glove.

What do you call an old snowman?
Water.

What do you call an evil chicken?
A deviled egg.

What do you call an avocado that's
been blessed by the pope?
Holy guacamole.

What do you call something that's
easy to get into, but hard to get out
of?
Trouble.

What do you call a redneck who's on
fire?
A firecracker.

What do you call two octopuses that
look exactly the same?
Itenticle.

What do you call the death of a man
who is hit by a falling ax?
Ax-idental.

What do you call the month that
soldiers hate the most?
March.

What do you call a sheep covered in
chocolate?
A candy baa.

What do you call a tiny mother?
A minimum.

What do you call leftover salad?
The last romaines.

What do you call an alligator with a vest?
An investigator.

What do you call the longest word in the dictionary?
Smiles – because there is a mile between each "s".

What do you call shaving a crazy sheep?
Shear madness.

What do you call the wife of a hippie?
A Mississippie.

What do you call something you can serve, but never eat?
A volleyball.

What do you call a factory that sells
OK products?
A satisfactory.

What do you call an Irish possum?
Opossum.

What do you call a pair of barracuda
fish?
A pairacuda.

What do you call a cross between a
kangaroo and a snake?
A jump rope.

What do you call a pay toilet?
Johnny Cash.

What do you call someone who is
working with a clock under his desk?
Working overtime.

What do you call a three-hundred pound tight end?
A wide receiver.

What do you call a joke you make in the morning while taking a shower?
A clean joke.

What do you call the driver who delivers Indian food?
A curryer.

What do you call the shoes that all spies wear?
Sneakers.

What do you call a Jedi with one arm?
Hand Solo.

What do you call the king of vegetables?

Elvis Parsley.

What do you call a piece of sad cheese?
Blue cheese.

What do you call a group of possums?
A possy.

What do you call a rabbit that is angry over getting burnt?
A hot cross bunny.

What do you call a dollar frozen in a big block of ice?
Cold hard cash.

What do you call a Russian tree?
Dimitree.

What do you call a dead skunk?
A stunk.

What do you call an otter with a brand
new pair of glasses?
A see otter.

What do you call a table that is next
to your bed?
A one-night stand.

What do you call a church that is on
fire?
Holy smokes.

What do you call a cross between a
porcupine and a turtle?
A slowpoke.

What do you call a magic owl?
Whoo-dini.

What do you call a magician on a plane?
A flying sorcerer.

What do you call an accountant who doesn't have a calculator?
Lost and lonely.

What do you call someone who is trying to catch a squirrel in a tree?
A nut.

What do you call a frog with no hind legs?
Unhoppy.

What do you call a deer with pink eye?
A colorful eye-deer.

What do you call something that always gets ahead?
A wig.

What do you call a chair that smokes weed?
A highchair.

What do you call a lazy baby kangaroo?
A pouch potato.

What do you call a ghost's true friend?
His ghoul-friend.

What do you call a turtle that keeps pooping everywhere?
Turdel.

What do you call lending money to a bison?
A buff-a-loan.

What do you call an acid with an attitude?
A mean-o-acid.

What do you call a cross between a tree and a baseball player?
Babe Root.

What do you call a boat full of polite soccer players?
A good sportsman ship.

What do you call that red stain around a shark's mouth?
Residude.

What do you call a paddle sale at the marina?
An oar deal.

What do you call a cross between a piece of paper and scissors?
Confetti.

What do you call a city of 20 million eggs?
New Yolk City.

What do you call a number that can't stay put?
A roamin' numeral.

What do you call it when you walk into a cafe you're sure you've been to before?
Deja brew.

What do you call a cross between a
donkey and a zebra?
A zeedonk.

What do you call an empty can of
Cheese Whiz?
Cheese Was.

What do you call an acrobat in shark-
infested waters?
A balanced breakfast.

What do you call a cross between a
baseball pitcher and a carpet?
A throw rug.

What do you call friends who love
math?
Algebros.

What do you call a month's worth of rain?
England.

What do you call a cat burrito?
A purrito.

What do you call a cross between two football teams and the Invisble Man?
A game of football like you've never seen before.

What do you call a terrorist who is good at baseball?
A Bronx Bomber.

What do you call a cute door?
Adorable.

What do call a cross between a frog
and a rabbit?
A bunny ribbit.

What do you call a woman who
crawls up walls?
Ivy.

What do you call a cross between a
pig and karate?
A porkchop.

What do you call an underwater spy?
James Pond.

What do you call a bathroom
superhero?
Flush Gordon.

What do you call a fairy in a
bathroom?
Stinkerbell.

What do you call it when a prisoner
takes his
own mugshot.
A cellfie.

What do you call it when someone
steals your morning coffee?
A mugging.

What do you call a Flamingo with
twenty toes?
A Flamingo.

ABOUT THE AUTHOR

ROBERT MYERS was born and raised in The Bronx, New York. He attended Baruch College (BA) and New Jersey City University (MA). Mr. Myers has been active in the creative and performing arts for six decades as an actor, model, and writer. He is the author of 365 KNOCK-KNOCK JOKES. Mr. Myers and his wife reside in New York City.

www.imdb.com/name/nm2827073

Printed in Great Britain
by Amazon